W9-BLI-613

Ambulances

by Marcia S. Freeman

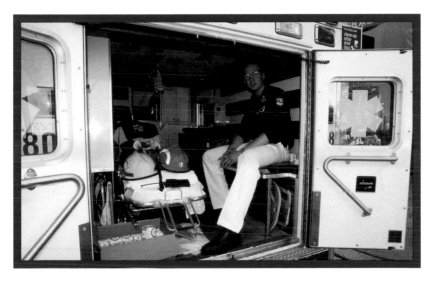

Consulting Editor:
Gail Saunders-Smith, Ph.D.

Consultant:
Mike Harmon
Administration Director
American Ambulance Association

Pebble Books

an imprint of Capstone Press
Mankato, Minnesota

Pebble Books are published by Capstone Press
151 Good Counsel Drive, P.O. Box 669, Mankato, Minnesota 56002
http://www.capstone-press.com

2 3 4 5 6 7 08 07 06 05 04 03

Library of Congress Cataloging-in-Publication Data
Freeman, Marcia S. (Marcia Sheehan), 1937–
    Ambulances / by Marcia S. Freeman.
    p. cm.—(Community vehicles)
    Includes bibliographical references and index.
    Summary: Describes ambulances, the equipment they carry, and the work they do.
    ISBN 0-7368-0100-6 (hardcover)
    ISBN 0-7368-8101-8 (paperback)
    1. Ambulances—Juvenile literature. [1. Ambulances.] I. Title. II. Series.
TL235.8.F74 1999
    616.02′5—dc21   98-4248

Note to Parents and Teachers

This series supports national social studies standards related to authority and government. This book describes and illustrates ambulances and the equipment they carry. The photographs support early readers in understanding the text. The sentence structures offer subtle challenges. This book introduces early readers to vocabulary used in this subject area. The vocabulary is defined in the Words to Know section. Early readers may need assistance in reading some words and in using the Table of Contents, Words to Know, Read More, Internet Sites, and Index/Word List sections of the book.

Table of Contents

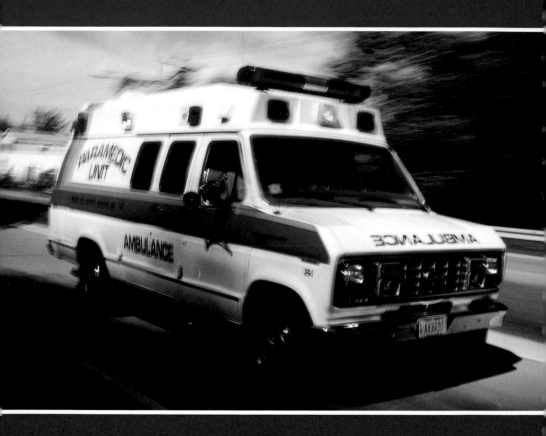

Ambulances travel fast.
Ambulances carry paramedics
and supplies. Paramedics use
the supplies to help sick and
hurt people.

Ambulances have lights that flash. Ambulances have sirens that make loud noises.

Lights and sirens warn people that ambulances are coming. Other drivers let ambulances pass them.

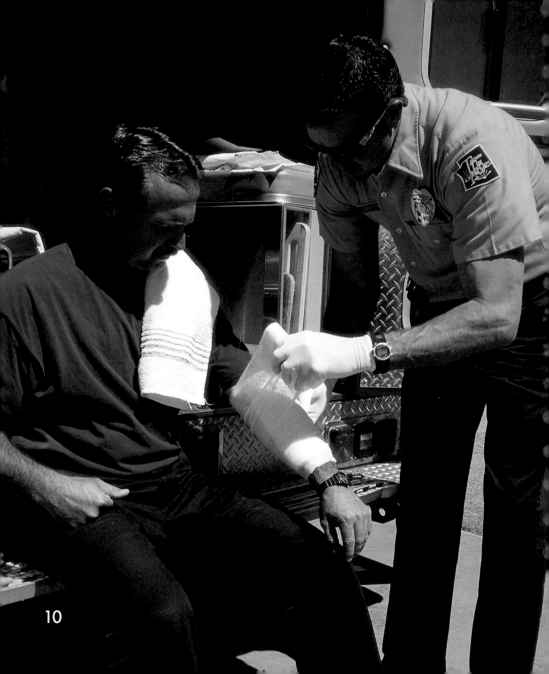

Ambulances carry bandages. Paramedics use bandages to cover cuts.

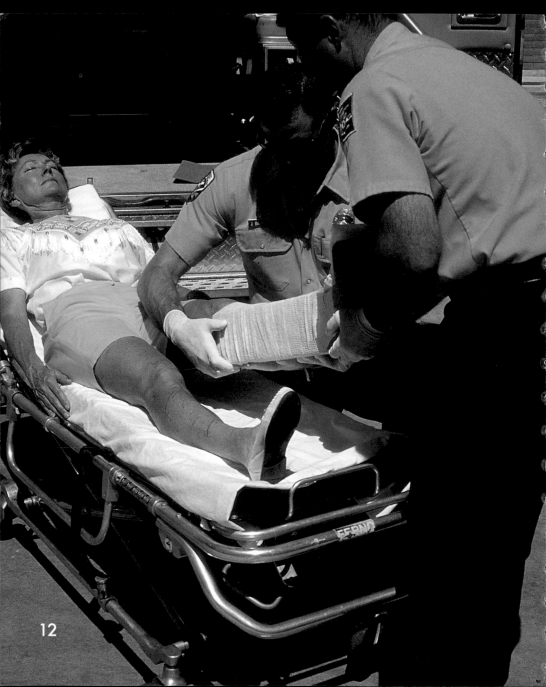

Ambulances carry splints. Paramedics use splints to hold broken bones in place.

Ambulances carry oxygen tanks. Paramedics use oxygen tanks to help people breathe.

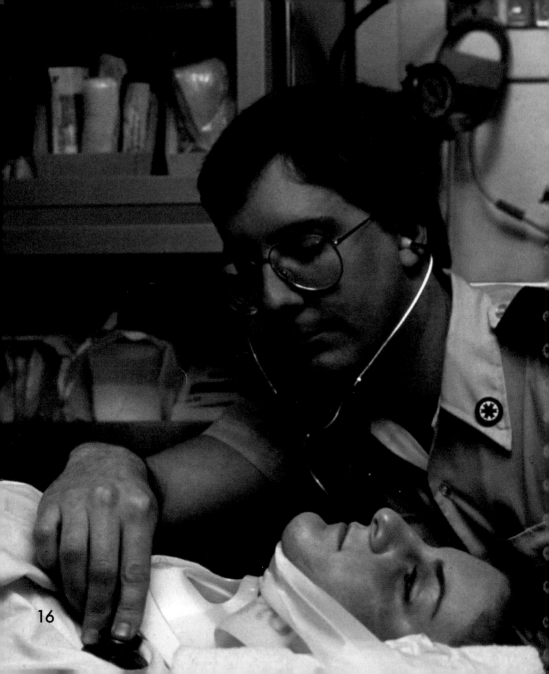

Ambulances carry stethoscopes. Paramedics use stethoscopes to hear people's hearts.

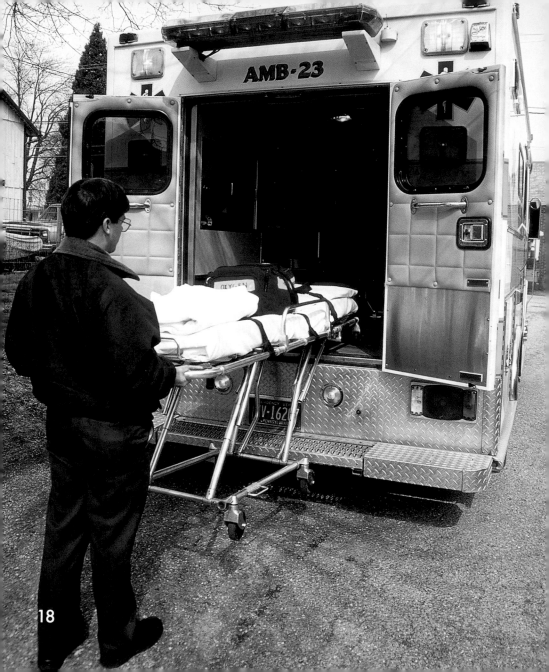
18

Ambulances carry stretchers. Paramedics use stretchers to move sick and hurt people to ambulances.

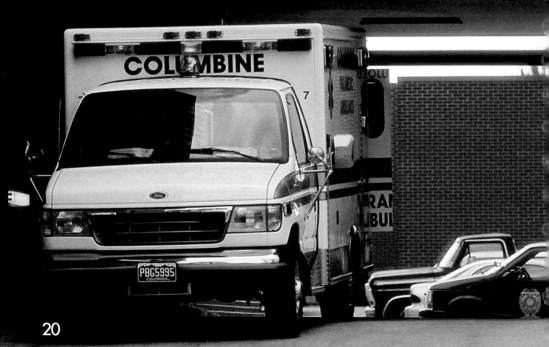

Ambulances take sick and hurt people to hospitals. Ambulances can travel to hospitals fast.

Words to Know

bandage—a piece of cloth that covers cuts and other wounds; bandages protect wounds.

oxygen—a gas that people need to breathe; ambulances carry oxygen in tanks.

paramedic—a person who treats sick and hurt people; paramedics travel in ambulances to places where people need treatment.

siren—a machine that makes a loud sound

splint—something used to keep hurt arms and legs straight; splints can be made from wood, metal, or plastic.

stethoscope—a tool used to listen to sounds inside a patient; people use stethoscopes to listen to hearts, lungs, and other body parts.

stretcher—something used to carry sick or hurt people; most ambulances have stretchers that look like beds on tall legs with wheels.

tank—a holder for air or liquid

Read More

Ethan, Eric. *Ambulances.* Emergency Vehicles. Milwaukee: G. Stevens Pub., 2002.

Hanson, Anne E. *Ambulances.* The Transportation Library. Mankato, Minn.: Bridgestone Books, 2001.

Internet Sites

Do you want to find out more about ambulances? Let FactHound, our fact-finding hound dog, do the research for you.

Here's how:

1) Visit *http://www.facthound.com*

2) Type in the **Book ID** number: **0736801006**

3) Click on **FETCH IT**.

FactHound will fetch Internet sites picked by our editors just for you!

Index/Word List

Word Count: 116
Early-Intervention Level: 16

Editorial Credits
Colleen Sexton, editor; Clay Schotzko/Icon Productions, cover designer;
   Sheri Gosewisch, photo researcher

Photo Credits
Borland Stock Photo/John S. Stewart, 16
Emergency!Stock/Howard M. Paul, 20
Images International/Erwin "Bud" Nielsen, 8, 10, 12
Maguire PhotoGraFX/Joseph P. Maguire, 14, 18
PhotoBank Inc., 6; Larry Mulvehill, 4
Unicorn Stock Photos/Tom McCarthy, 1
Visuals Unlimited/Arthur R. Hill, cover